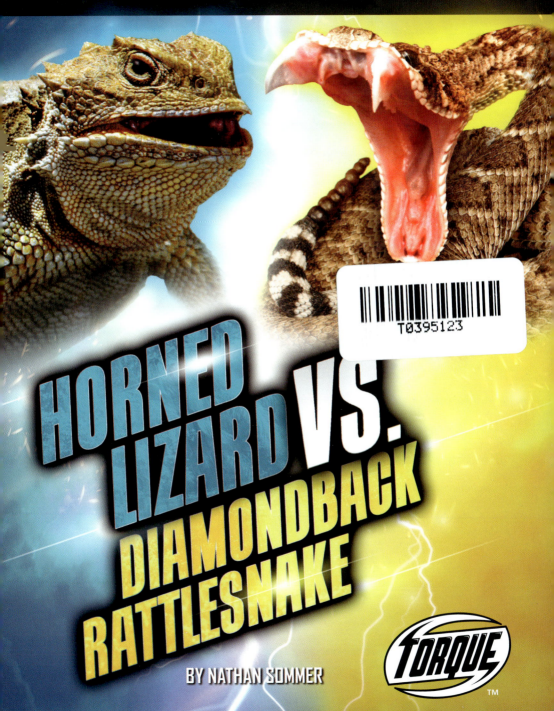

ANIMAL BATTLES

HORNED LIZARD VS. DIAMONDBACK RATTLESNAKE

BY NATHAN SOMMER

BELLWETHER MEDIA • MINNEAPOLIS, MN

Torque brims with excitement perfect for thrill-seekers of all kinds. Discover daring survival skills, explore uncharted worlds, and marvel at mighty engines and extreme sports. In *Torque* books, anything can happen. Are you ready?

This edition first published in 2026 by Bellwether Media, Inc.

No part of this publication may be reproduced in whole or in part without written permission of the publisher. For information regarding permission, write to Bellwether Media, Inc., Attention: Permissions Department, 3500 American Blvd W, Suite 150, Bloomington, MN 55431.

Library of Congress Cataloging-in-Publication Data

LC record for Horned Lizard vs. Diamondback Rattlesnake available at: https://lccn.loc.gov/2025012855

Text copyright © 2026 by Bellwether Media, Inc. TORQUE and associated logos are trademarks and/or registered trademarks of Bellwether Media, Inc. Bellwether Media is a division of FlutterBee Education Group.

Editor: Suzane Nguyen   Designer: Josh Brink

Printed in the United States of America, North Mankato, MN.

TABLE OF CONTENTS

THE COMPETITORS	4
SECRET WEAPONS	10
ATTACK MOVES	16
READY, FIGHT!	20
GLOSSARY	22
TO LEARN MORE	23
INDEX	24

THE COMPETITORS

The grasslands of North America are home to many dangerous **predators**. Horned lizards have special defenses to stay safe.

The lizards sometimes live near diamondback rattlesnakes. These snakes are deadly predators that use super senses to find **prey**. What happens when these two **reptiles** come face-to-face?

Horned lizards have wide, flat bodies. Many horned lizards are reddish brown or gray. Pointy scales line their backs. Their name comes from the horns on top of their heads.

There are many kinds of horned lizards. They live in deserts and grasslands throughout North and Central America.

HORNED LIZARD PROFILE

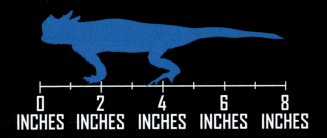

| 0 INCHES | 2 INCHES | 4 INCHES | 6 INCHES | 8 INCHES |

LENGTH
UP TO 8 INCHES
(20.3 CENTIMETERS)

WEIGHT
UP TO 5.3 OUNCES
(150 GRAMS)

HABITATS

GRASSLANDS

DESERTS

MOUNTAINS

HORNED LIZARD RANGE

■ RANGE

WESTERN DIAMONDBACK RATTLESNAKE PROFILE

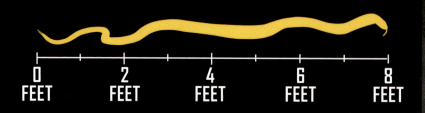

| 0 FEET | 2 FEET | 4 FEET | 6 FEET | 8 FEET |

LENGTH
UP TO 8 FEET
(2.4 METERS)

WEIGHT
UP TO 14.7 POUNDS
(6.7 KILOGRAMS)

HABITATS

GRASSLANDS

DESERTS

MOUNTAINS

WESTERN DIAMONDBACK RATTLESNAKE RANGE

■ RANGE

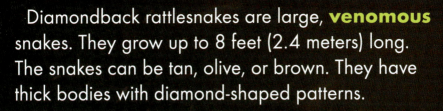

Diamondback rattlesnakes are large, **venomous** snakes. They grow up to 8 feet (2.4 meters) long. The snakes can be tan, olive, or brown. They have thick bodies with diamond-shaped patterns.

Diamondback rattlesnakes live in grasslands, deserts, and mountains. They are found in the southern United States and parts of Mexico. They often hide underground during the day. They hunt at night.

SECRET WEAPONS

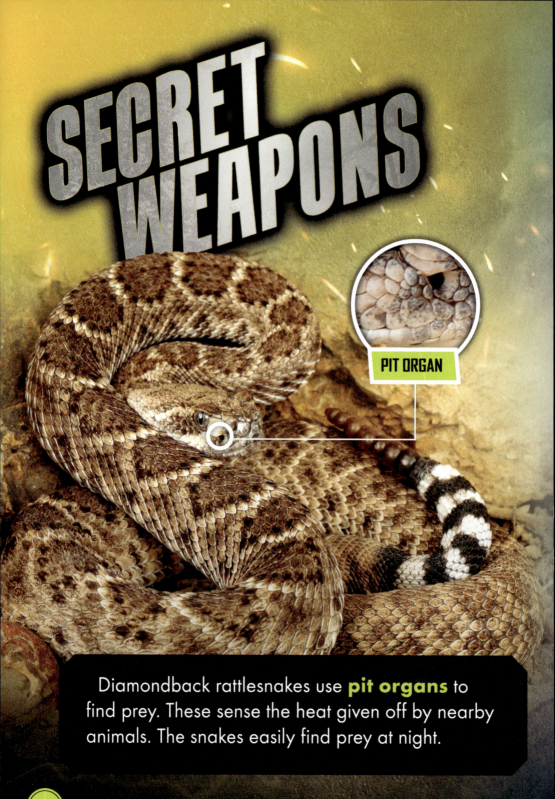

PIT ORGAN

Diamondback rattlesnakes use **pit organs** to find prey. These sense the heat given off by nearby animals. The snakes easily find prey at night.

HORNED LIZARD BLOOD SPRAYING DISTANCE

5 FEET (1.5 METERS)

| 0 FEET | 1 FOOT | 2 FEET | 3 FEET | 4 FEET | 5 FEET |

Horned lizards can spray blood from their eyes! They burst **blood vessels** in their eyes. Then blood sprays out. The bad taste of the blood often surprises enemies.

Horned lizards use **camouflage** to hunt and hide. They quickly change colors to easily match their surroundings. This makes them hard for both predators and prey to spot.

DIAMONDBACK RATTLESNAKE VENOM SPEED

HOW FAST IT WORKS = 1 SECOND

Diamondback rattlesnakes have deadly bites. Their large, sharp fangs **inject** prey with venom. The deadly venom works fast to defeat the animals.

SECRET WEAPONS

HORNED LIZARD

SPRAYS BLOOD

CAMOUFLAGE

SPIKY, PUFFED-UP BODIES

Horned lizards suck in air to puff up their spiky bodies. This makes them look bigger! The **scare tactic** often makes them look too large for enemies to eat.

DIAMONDBACK RATTLESNAKE

SECRET WEAPONS

PIT ORGANS

VENOM

RATTLES

BEHIND THE RATTLE

Rattlesnake rattles are made of hollow scales that are loosely connected.

Diamondback rattlesnakes are named after their tail rattles. They quickly shake their tails to make a buzzing sound. This noise warns enemies to stay away.

ATTACK MOVES

Horned lizards are **ambush hunters**. They hide and wait for bugs to walk by. Then they use their sticky tongues to catch them! Most prey is swallowed whole.

LIVING PREY
Horned lizards only eat live prey.

Diamondback rattlesnakes lie still until prey comes close. Pit organs help them sense exactly where prey is. Then they quickly bite the animal with their fangs!

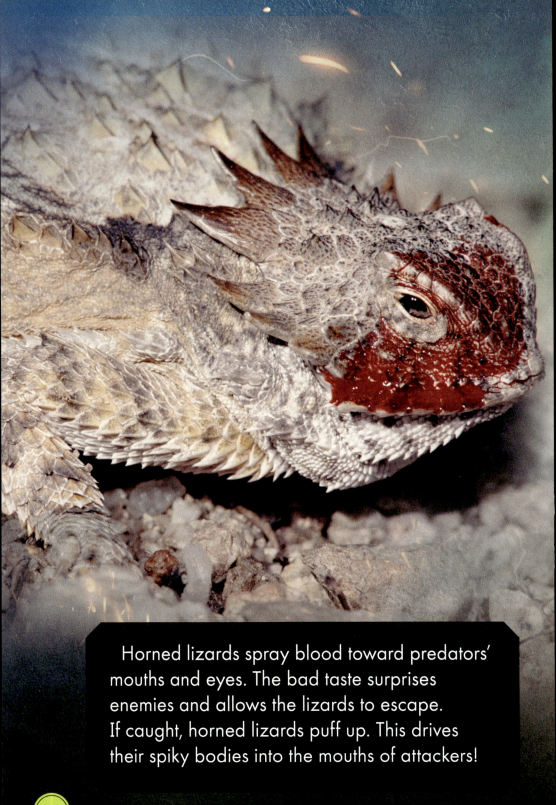

Horned lizards spray blood toward predators' mouths and eyes. The bad taste surprises enemies and allows the lizards to escape. If caught, horned lizards puff up. This drives their spiky bodies into the mouths of attackers!

Diamondback rattlesnakes are **aggressive**. They **coil** their bodies and rattle their tails when threatened. They bite if enemies do not go away.

LIGHTNING QUICK

Diamondback rattlesnakes can strike in under one second.

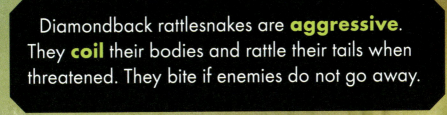

READY, FIGHT!

A horned lizard lies still while hunting. Suddenly, it spots a diamondback rattlesnake. The lizard quickly changes colors to hide. But the snake's pit organs sense heat from the lizard.

The snake quickly bites. The lizard sprays blood from its eyes. But it is quickly defeated by the snake's venom. Nothing gets past this diamondback rattlesnake!

GLOSSARY

aggressive—ready to fight

ambush hunters—animals that sit and wait to catch their prey

blood vessels—connected tubes that pump blood throughout the body

camouflage—colors and patterns used to help an animal hide in its surroundings

coil—to wrap around in a spiral

inject—to force a fluid into something

pit organs—special body parts that allow snakes to detect the movements of prey in darkness

predators—animals that hunt other animals for food

prey—animals that are hunted by other animals for food

reptiles—cold-blooded animals that have backbones and lay eggs

scare tactic—a fighting strategy in which one animal tries to make itself appear as large or scary as possible in hopes of scaring the other off

venomous—able to produce venom; venom is a kind of poison made by some snakes.

TO LEARN MORE

AT THE LIBRARY

Boutland, Craig. *Western Diamondback Rattlesnake.* Minneapolis, Minn.: Bearport Publishing, 2021.

Hudd, Emily. *Texas Horned Lizards.* North Mankato, Minn.: Capstone Press, 2020.

Wilson, Libby. *Rattlesnakes.* Mendota Heights, Minn.: Apex Editions, 2023.

ON THE WEB

Factsurfer.com gives you a safe, fun way to find more information.

1. Go to www.factsurfer.com

2. Enter "horned lizard vs. diamondback rattlesnake" into the search box and click 🔍.

3. Select your book cover to see a list of related content.

INDEX

ambush hunters, 16
bites, 13, 17, 19, 21
blood, 11, 18, 21
bodies, 6, 9, 19
camouflage, 12
Central America, 6
coil, 19
colors, 6, 9, 12, 20
eyes, 11, 18, 21
fangs, 13, 17
habitat, 4, 6, 7, 8, 9
hide, 9, 12, 16, 20
horns, 6
hunt, 9, 12, 20
Mexico, 9
night, 9, 10
North America, 4, 6
pit organs, 10, 17, 20

predators, 4, 5, 12, 18
prey, 5, 10, 12, 13, 16, 17
range, 4, 6, 7, 8, 9
rattles, 15, 19
reptiles, 5
scales, 6, 15
scare tactic, 14
size, 7, 8, 9, 14
spiky bodies, 14, 18
spray, 11, 18, 21
strike, 19
tails, 15, 19
tongues, 16
United States, 9
venomous, 9, 13, 21
weapons, 14, 15

The images in this book are reproduced through the courtesy of: Universal Images/ SuperStock, front cover (short-horned lizard); Audrey Snider-Bell, front cover (diamondback rattlesnake), pp. 10, 15 (pit organs); piemags/nature/ Alamy, pp. 2-3, 20-21, 22-24 (lizard); Rich Wagner/ Alamy, pp. 2-3, 20-21, 22-24 (rattlesnake); eshma/ AdobeStock, pp. 2-3, 20-21, 22-24; Juniors Bildarchiv / F304/ Alamy, p. 4; Chronicle/ Alamy, p. 5; WD Suncrest, pp. 6-7; Koshevnyk, p. 7 (lizard icon); Save nature and wildlife, p. 8 (snake icon); JohnPitcher/ Getty, pp. 8-9; Alexander Wong, p. 10 (pit organ); John Cancalosi/ Alamy/ Nature Picture Library, pp. 11, 18; PetlinDmitry, p. 11 (vector horned lizard); Danita Delimont/ Alamy, p. 12; Wasantha/ AdobeStock, p. 13 (snake venom graphic); FotoIdee, p. 13 (time clock); McDonald Wildlife Photography Inc./ Getty, p. 13; Gerald C. Kelley/ Science Source Images, p. 14; LM OTERO/ AP Images, p. 14 (sprays blood); Jon G. Fuller/VWPics/ Alamy, p. 14 (camouflage) (spiky, puffed up body); storytold, p. 15 (venom); Spineback, p. 15 (rattles); tomreichner/ AdobeStock, p. 15; R. Van Nostrand/ Science Source Images, p. 16; Stan Tekiela Author / Naturalist / Wildlife Photographer/ Getty, p. 17; Chase D'Animulls/ AdobeStock, p. 19.